The Woman With A
by
Anne Walsh D

First published 2019 by Fly on the Wall Poetry Press

Published in the UK by
Fly on the Wall Poetry Press
56 High Lea Rd
New Mills
Derbyshire
SK22 3DP

www.flyonthewallpoetry.co.uk

ISBN: 978-1-9995986-4-8

Copyright © 2019

978-1-9995986-4-8

A CIP Catalogue record for this book is available from the British Library.

To Brian and Hannah, for your loving acceptance.

Contents

Acknowledgements

Thanks to the editors of the journals, in which some of these poems (or forms of them) originally appeared: *Ariel Chart, Blue Nib, Boyne Berries, Cauldron LGBT+ Anthology, Cránnog, Dodging the Rain, Heart and Humanity, The Irish Times* and *Star 82 Review.*

Many thanks to poets who read and gave feedback on some of these poems at various stages, in particular, Isabelle Kenyon, Kevin Higgins, participants in the Over the Edge online workshops, members of the Museum writer's group and the members of my poetry family aka the online group Poets Abroad.

Special thanks to my parents, my brothers and to three extraordinary women who have witnessed and supported my journey: Mai, Marina and Marie.

Guide to Becoming a Writer

Be the first to scramble out of Mam's womb.
Play Cowboys and Indians with your brothers. Dump Barbie.

Be left-handed. Pretend to write with your other hand in school.
Lefties are evil, according to Sister Concepta in Junior Infants.

Become addicted to Enid Blyton. Adventures with the Famous Five
are more exciting than playing with snotty-nosed Niamh's gang.

Listen to "All By Myself," on your Walkman until the tape breaks.
Fantasise about your latest crush drawing rings around your nipples.

Get six A's in your Leaving Cert, pursue the degree your career
guidance teacher tells you will guarantee a pensionable job.

Fall in love for the first time. Get dumped. Consider walking across
O'Connell Street on a foggy morning without the little green man.

Have a mid-twenties crisis, chuck the well-paid job, backpack around
the world. Keep a travel diary. Don't ever let your mother read it.

Race towards "being settled," in your thirties, get promoted at work,
meet your soulmate. Realise later there's no such thing.

Marry, get pregnant, give birth.
Enjoy being a "happy family," for the next five minutes.

Leave him, make-up, go back. Repeat twice.
Separate, get your own car, house, and life.

Go see a therapist. When she tells you to start writing - Just Do It.
Your sessions give you meat for a memoir that will never get published.

Enjoy the benefits of being single. Switch on the bedside light
in the middle of the night and write without anybody to interrupt.

Acquire a chronic illness, endure the pain it inflicts.
Hold your breath as smog blinds and chokes. Stop writing.

Think of your children when life becomes unbearable.
You'll never become a real writer if you jump into the river.

Convince yourself the world needs your poems.
Gobble the anti-depressants. Start writing again.

Tawny Owl

Each night after my husband fell asleep
and the moon was full
I'd gaze from the bedroom window
at the tawny owl
perched on the barn's roof.

Moving a hand up my thigh,
I'd dream of laying my head
on her feathered mound.

Moving my other hand,
down my arched neck,
I'd dream of holding her breast
in my palm, her breath,
moistening my desert skin.

Sometimes I opened the window to listen
to her melody of "Tu-woo's,"
before husband shoved himself inside.

In daylight I milked cows,
pulled eggs from bottoms of stubborn hens,
fed motherless lambs.

One November morning
I found my owl,
her limp body,
floating face down
in the duck pond.
I cawed like an old crow.

Cúchulainn

In mid-life I grew into my childhood hero.
I stood in the hound's shadow. Its paws,
like circular saw blades,
poised, ready to maul.

I gripped my hurley in one hand,
sliothair in the other,
wished it was only a mythical dog
I had to kill.

The hound's jaws were prised apart
by verbal battles and egg-shelled
silences. Its hot breath
raised blisters on my skin.

I whacked the sliothair
down its gullet, watched
as the ball dragged the entrails
of my marriage out the rear end.

I grabbed his hind legs, smashed the body
against a concrete wall, became sole guardian
of the vulnerable. The ones,
I believed hound would always protect.

Cúchulainn was an Irish mythological hero. He gained his name after killing Culann's fierce guard-dog in self-defence and offered to take its place until a replacement could be reared.

Hamster

Even a shot of WD40,
didn't stop her treadmill creaking.
The noise made her ears twitch
as if she had been electrocuted.

My hamster was not one
for giving up. Her little legs
kept running on that bloody
treadmill, until it broke.

She dragged her flabby body
to a corner, crouched and folded
in on herself, a blackish-grey
mound of fluff.

When my husband stuck his finger,
through the wiry bars and poked
her to perform, she didn't know
how to tell him – she was broken.

History of My Sexual Encounters

*All penises in this poem are fictitious, any resemblance to real penises,
dying or dead, is purely coincidental.*

The Donegal man who I'm convinced was gay
Penis like a prize winning sausage dog
Didn't want to struggle with my stubble
For fear of taking the shine off his coat.

A Bristol boy, ripped my hymen
Penis like a Twister ice lolly
Always melted too quickly
And never quite filled me.

The Aussie Naval Officer
Penis as long & bent as the steel arches
Of Sydney Harbour Bridge
I jumped before he stood to salute.

The bushman in Kakadu
Penis tasted like a burnt kangaroo steak
Said he hates when the Sheila's don't come.
Takes a bit longer than five minutes, bucko.

The Dub I met in Singapore
Penis, slick as Tiger Beer easing down a parched throat
He wanted me to go down - south on a boat to Darwin
I flew north to Kathmandu.

Finally the Wexford Wanker
Held his penis as if it were a fishing rod
Caught my clitoris, reeled me in
Took me seven years, to escape his hook.

Vows

I do, he said.

He also said,

I'll give up smoking for Lent.
Just going to town for cigarettes, won't be long.

Battery in my phone died.
I won't be going to the pub after the baby's born.

I only went for a fast one to wet the baby's head.
Got delayed, Dad needed a hand pulling a calf.

I didn't do it to hurt you.
It was only a few calls to chat lines.

There's nothing wrong with our marriage.
It's all in your head. You're depressed.

You're an ass. A bitch.
Can't please you, no matter what I do.

I'll burn the house down if you leave.
Top myself, then you'll get nothing.

I can't afford to pay you maintenance.
You've destroyed our family.

At the courthouse door, he said,

Come home, the loneliness is killing me.

To My Fifty-year-old Self

Unclasp your bra
   let
      it
         fall.

Ease your comfy cotton knickers down your legs.

Look at your naked self
untouched
by another for seven years.

Hold your breasts.
Watch them spill out of your hands.

Run your thumbs along the curved waterslide of your spine.

Massage the hollow between your hips
smooth as a leaf in late summer.

Cradle your belly.

Admire the way it protrudes over greying hair
framed by the Y of your thighs.

Play a sonata on your skin
stiffen your nipples
close your eyes.

Dive into

The Dream of the Fisherman's Wife

Coming Out to My Therapist

Ok, I'm attracted to women BUT I'm not gay.

She raises her glass, takes a sip and asks,
Are straight women attracted to other women?

It's just a phase, I'm going through. It'll pass.

She shifts in her seat, leans forward,
Have you ever heard of internalized homophobia?

I grip the arms of my chair,
I'm not anti-gay and I'm not one of them either.

Her Hug

stirs my bulb heart
in the same way
my ex-husband's did.

Her perfume   Daisy
coaxes my foetal flower.
It pushes upwards
through a hair follicle
in my skin.

Her heat
unfolds the bud.
My Daisy blooms.

Through her lips
blows a breeze softer
than bog-cotton.

Pollen dusts my cheek
like dry mustard.

I let a sliver
of white petal
touch her forehead;
glide downwards
towards her mouth.

Her face buckles
as if slapped by
the bumper of a 4X4.

I swallow my kiss.
Burns my throat.
Petals wilt.
Retreat.

It's Not Easy Being a Woman

I throw Barbie into the slurry tank
watch the cow shite gobble her up,
get a clatter on the arse from Daddy.

Blood leaks from my privates.
Breasts bob all over the place
when I'm playing football with the boys.

Jim kisses me on our second date
his dick rubs against my thigh
my friends say, he's a ride.

He asks me to marry him
I'm fed up of Mammy's nagging
my friends say, he's a ride.

I pretend he's Pammie from Baywatch
when he fucks me, I even moan
just like she does.

I give birth to three boys
listen to their first cries,
Jim wets their heads with a pint.

He crashes the car
on the way home from the pub.
I milk cows as well as cook dinners.

Cow's calving, I call the new vet.
After the birth, I notice
she wears the same perfume as mine.

It won't be easy, being a lesbian.

Coming Out to Myself

I stare at the waitress in Costa, vulva twitching,

She has a fine pair of breasts.
I'd love to hold them in my hands.
And look at her bum in those skinny jeans.
No wedding ring either.
Reminds me of my teacher in fifth class.

Fuck...I am one of them.

Friesian

The new vet's perfume
cut through the shite in the shed.
She pulled on shoulder-length gloves,
reached inside my best dairy cow

up through the birth canal.
The animal roared like a chainsaw
until in a whoosh of blood,
a Friesian calf slipped out.

After the calf had suckled
I asked the new vet in for tea,
released my copper-highlighted hair
from its ponytail while she washed.

The first time we made love
her hands delivered me from my labour days.
Like my Friesian calf, I landed
on sweet-smelling straw.

Metamorphosis

After Franz Kafka

I lie in her arms
breasts pressed against my back;
listen to her soft snores.

She doesn't see the demon pest
in me, its reddish-brown shell,
insect head and large black eyes.

She doesn't feel its wax coated
exoskeleton or the claws
attached to my legs.

I manoeuvre myself out of bed
scurry towards the bathroom
into the shower.

Boiling water lashes my vermin
armour. I cry cockroach tears
stiff wings dissolve

antennae swirl down the drain.
Six spindly legs
become two again.

Grafton Street on a Saturday Evening

A chat over coffee defibrillates
our hearts. Fingers interlock
for the first time.

We leave the warmth
of Bewley's café. January
drizzle dances in her hair.

Roses, Irises, Chrysanthemums
stuffed into black plastic buckets
lean towards us.

We dodge on-coming pedestrians.
Curse hooded teenagers
forging a gap between us.

We recoup, cross the paved street,
notes of Hot Chocolate
from another café tempt.

Taxi rank.
Damn no queue.

My glossed lips stick to hers
blue eyes on green
chests tighten.
Ambulance sirens in ears,
perfect storms in stomachs,
hands joined like Siamese twins
separate,
open the car door.

"Heuston Station, please."

Coming Out to My Son

Mam, do you have a girlfriend?
he asks,
piercing me with don't-lie-to-me eyes.

Yes.
Is she just a friend with benefits?
No.
Is it just a phase you are going through?
No.

His acned cheek touches my forehead
his gangly arms wrap around my shoulders.
Same as his toddler arms used to, but different.

Thank you, I whisper.
I was just fishing, he says.
You thought you'd hook a goldfish, instead you caught a pike.
No, I caught a whale.

Being in Love at Fifty

plucks me from death row,
as fingers go deep into wet vulvas
& lips suck dry nipples. Hands expunge
the curdled cream & bitter fruit
from my body. Our medley of skin & bones
sink into a bowl of Eton Mess.

Being in love at fifty
makes me wonder if Eros will crumble
like Wensleydale cheese
or taste like Blue Stilton, after a year or two,
or if it can be transformed
into the perfect soufflé.

Being in love at fifty
makes me cry, my daughter's image
of me creases, feels like
she's lost Santa all over again
has to make room for someone else
to sit beside her in my heart.

Being in love at fifty
makes me grin, my shopping bag
contains a birthday card
& polyester shirt for my daughter
to give to her father. Lying on top,
a cerise lace bra for my lover.

Lesbia

After Catullus

Our love will vaccinate against the germs,
others vomit from their mouldy mouths.
They will not stop me gazing at your body,
in the bedside lamp's low light.
My fingers will rest in the hollow
of your lower back. Tongue
will tip yours, taste Cabernet.
Your hands will roam & find home.
Our coupling will gather momentum
on ivory sheets until the bulb blows.
Tears will trail down my cheeks.
We'll spoon each other to sleep;
wake in an hour for more.

Ache of Naked Bodies

Yours and mine
in the tallboy mirror.
Soaped skin,
pliable as dough,
rises, coils.
We braid our bodies.

Perfume,
yours and mine
embrace, seeps
into our pores.
Summer sighs escape
from every orifice.

We lick fingertips,
dipped,
in salmon flesh
knowing they feed
our rare fusions.

Someone to Watch over Me

In the midst of our kissing, my eyelids closed.
She lay awake, tracking my sleeping breath
her hands walked the weedy path
around the girth of my body

stroked mottled skin as if it were cat fur.
An hour later I woke
underside of my damp thigh resting on hers
my face nestled in the valley

between her jaw and collarbone.
Before I could say sorry, she whispered,
"I love watching you sleep."
Her fingers massaged my scalp.

I moved my head so my cheek
rested on hers, sleek as a laurel leaf,
remnants of her moisturiser
as potent as a newly flowered peony.

I couldn't remember the last time
someone watched over me.

Coming Out to My Daughter

I have something to tell you.
Don't wanna know, she says, scrolling her Instagram feed.

It's good news, I'm seeing someone.
Boyfriend or girlfriend.
Girl.

Her head rises from her phone screen.
That's okay. I always knew you were gay.
At least now, you won't be lonely when I go to college.

The Dublin Expressway

will stop outside the village
post office. I'll alight, heave backpack
over my shoulder. Unfinished essay
on "The Rise of the Suffragettes"
in its side pocket.

Before I trudge the mile home
I'll stop into Betty's and buy you
twenty Benson and Hedges,
an apology for not being down since Christmas.

My new Docs Martins will burn the skin
around my ankles as I walk.
I'll pause and watch lambs leap over clumps
of bulrushes in a field. Their mothers will glare
and bleat. Seanie, aboard his new Massey Ferguson
will stop to offer a lift.
I'll decline.

When I open our farmyard gate
the cattle in the slatted house will low,
pigs grunt. The smell of silage
will make me nauseous. I'll be relieved
if Dad is still at the mart.

I'll leave backpack in the scullery,
open the kitchen door. You'll say,
hello stranger, and continue to prick holes
in the raw apple tart.

I'll make a pot of tea.
After you put the tart in the oven
I'll give you the cigarettes and say,

"Mam, I want to tell you something."

Your ash will fall on the floured table,
as I extract the over-cooked words lodged in my gut.
When I finish, the whirr of the oven's electric fan,
will be the only sound to fill the room.

You'll smoke three cigarettes in quick succession,
tea going cold. Then you'll look out at the herd
of clouds trampling across the sky.
Cat will scratch the kitchen pane and hiss
when you open the window, tell her to scat.

Burnt pastry will pollute the air, sting our eyes.
You'll grab a tea towel, yank the oven door,
pull the apple tart out and dump it in the bin.
You'll turn to me and say,
"Well at least you're not pregnant.
Say nothing to your father, he hates waste."

After a pause and wipe of your ploughed brow,
you'll pick up the rolling pin and last lump of pastry.

Coming Out to My Mother

I'm seeing someone, it's a woman.

Her eyes still on the TV screen, she says,
your father was wondering why you got your hair cut so short.
I'm glad you have company.

She presses the volume button on the remote,
bit harder than needed.

Oh ... that's terrible, she says,
now they think blood pressure tablets are carcinogenic.
I'd better ring the doctor tomorrow.

From Chink to Rio Grande Rift

For years I dozed on my bed,
unaware of diverging tectonic plates under me,
like those that created the Mid-Atlantic Ridge.
They split body and mind.

Liquid rock bubbled like a witch's cauldron.
I clutched my midriff, told myself it was an ulcer.
The pressure fractured my base, rising
magma burned dikes in my flesh.

Lava formed sills on my surface,
flushed my cheeks. Just as my plates
were supposed to settle and glide into old age
a woman's touch smashed my crust.

My amber core exposed, I roared like a lioness,
volcanic ash scratched my throat.
I hoped my mother would survive
the lava bomb that missiled towards home
and imagined her thinking if she'd given me a sister

instead of five brothers
I wouldn't have turned out this way.
Lover and I drifted into sleep
an ash-grey cloud over our entangled limbs.
I dreamed of the priest, who once said,

as he flexed his fingers, masturbation causes blindness;
making love is for making babies
and gays are intrinsically disordered.
My brain, marinated in doctrine, castigated
me for not keeping the eruption underground.

Coming Out to My Father

Did Mam tell you my news?
He adjusts his hearing aid.

What?
Did Mam tell you my news?

No.
I'm seeing someone.
Oh. Is it a man?
No. A woman.

He opens his newspaper, flicks through the pages,
and says, England are doing well in the World Cup.

Later, cryptic crossword completed,
he puts his pencil on the table, turns to me,

you were my daughter the day you were born
and you're still my daughter.

Mná na hÉireann (Women of Ireland)

To die not having known the frenzy
of making love with a woman
is to live without ever jumping
over the bar of your crib.

How could you not want
to watch a woman fling her underwear
on your bedroom floor
present you with soft skin

for your nails and teeth
to score like blades on dough.
How could you not want
to feel your edges

slip into her hollows, like a spoon
folding flour into cake batter.
How could you not want
to hear her whimper,

crescendo to a jungle roar
while your fingers move inside her.
How could you not want
a denouement to your play,

when secret stories leak onto ivory sheets
then tease tongues and start the sequel.
How could you not want
to drag a woman to bed

at seven on a Saturday evening
rise at two on Sunday afternoon,
sleep-deprived
and smelling like a marathon runner,

race outside to tackle
weedy flower beds
gleeful that soil will not rest
in your clipped fingernails.

I Clutch at Love

Pull her udder
suckle hot milk from shriveled teats
grasp the bars of her keratin horns
before they gouge my abdomen

brush my cheek against her hide
cry while she bellows
corral her in the rushy field
lay myself bare

for her hooves to stomp
and mulch me to muck
grab her hocks
before she breaks through briars

bring her to her knees
load her onto a truck
drive to the abattoir,
watch her blood flood my feet.

No More Fairy Tales

Tattooist inked the skin
on my abdomen.
A green dragon emerged, lounging
in a balloon's wicker basket.

He exhaled hot air upwards.
The needle's scratchy pain
subsided as the balloon inflated
and floated towards my breast.

Your tales said dragons
were dangerous. Mine kept me afloat
in skies of dark dodgem clouds
and white-water rapid rain.

When tattooist finished,
the dragon had swallowed
an ex's once indelible name.
In my story I save the princess,

she tickles my balloon, palms
the basket, licks my dragon's
amber breath without guarantee
of a happy-ever-anything.

Self-love

After Mary Oliver

If you feel your heart leap
when you glimpse your face
in the kitchen window

admire the faint image that is you
feast on your beauty

don't think of self-love
as a crumb you must blow
from your table

think of it as the yeast
that will develop your dough
think of how it will nourish you

to rise

      again
           again
                and
                    again.

I Have Lived

In his body
Grazed my hand on his stubbly head
Lost myself in his rainforest armpits
Sheltered under the ledge of his chin
Roamed the plains of his chest like a nomad
Swirled his Jack Daniels in my mouth
Ran with bulls through his fields of desire
Oiled my iron walls to ease his entrance.

In her body
Grasped her bleached marram grass
Surfed her peaks and troughs
Licked maple syrup from her lips
Bathed naked in her volcanic springs
Settled my cheek on the inside of her thigh
Sipped her dry gin
Let her light a candle in my cave.

What is there left to explore?

Author Biography

Anne Walsh Donnelly is a single mother of two teenage children and lives in the west of Ireland. Her work has been published in several literary outlets including *The Irish Times, Crannóg, Boyne Berries, The Blue Nib, Cold Coffee Stand, Ariel, Heart and Humanity, Inside the Bell Jar, Please Hear What I'm Not Saying* and *Star82 Review.*

Her short stories have been shortlisted in competitions such as the *Over the Edge New Writer of the Year Award* (2014 & 2016), *Fish International Prize* (2015) and the *RTÉ Radio One Frances Mac Manus competition* (2014 & 2015). Her poems were highly commended in the *Over the Edge New Writer of the Year Award* (2017 & 2018). She won the Winter/Spring 2017/2018 *Blue Nib* poetry chapbook competition and also the 2018 *Over the Edge Fiction Slam.* She was also nominated for the Pushcart Prize in 2018.

Her debut short story collection will be published in September 2019.

Social Media:

Facebook:
AnneWalshDonnelly

Twitter:
@AnneWDonnelly

Instagram:
annewalshdonnellypoetry

About Fly on the Wall Press:

A publisher with a conscience.
Publishing high quality anthologies on pressing issues, chapbooks and poetry products, from exceptional poets around the globe.
Founded in 2018 by founding editor, Isabelle Kenyon.

Other publications:

Please Hear What I'm Not Saying (February 2018. Anthology, profits to Mind.)
Persona Non Grata (October 2018. Anthology, profits to Shelter and Crisis Aid UK.)
Bad Mommy/Stay Mommy by Elisabeth Horan (May 2019. Chapbook.)

Social Media:

@fly_press (Twitter)
@flyonthewall_poetry (Instagram)
@flyonthewallpoetry (Facebook)
www.flyonthewallpoetry.co.uk